Homeless, not Invisible

photography documentary
by
Sharon Rodriguez

Homeless, not Invisible

photography documentary by

Sharon Rodriguez

EMP
Kansas City, MO
EMPbooks.com

Copyright © 2017 by Sharon Rodriguez

All rights reserved. No part of this book may be reproduced, scanned, or distributed in any printed or electronic form, including information storage and retrieval systems, without permission. Please do not participate in or encourage piracy of copyrighted materials in violation of the author's rights. Please purchase only authorized editions.

First Edition: 10 9 8 7 6 5 4 3 2 1

ISBN: 978-0-9985077-3-6

Library of Congress Control Number: 2017941631

Design, Layout: Jeanette Powers
all photos/text: Sharon Rodriguez

INTRODUCTION

Homeless? In Johnson County, Kansas?

How can that be?
The county is the most affluent in the state of Kansas.

I first saw a bright blue tarp shaped like a tent in a park where I walk. I found out there were homeless living in that park. I started asking questions. Why do they live in the park? Aren't there places that house them?

Being a photographer, I decided to start a Photography Documentary to capture these homeless people. I put gloves and hats in the park so I could see them when they came out to get the items. They were gone by the time I got back to them. I asked several of the charities in Johnson County where they were living. I walked through the woods to find evidence of their living quarters. I was getting frustrated.

I had a break one day when I was coming home from a meeting. I saw a man walking toward the Olathe Library. I stopped and watched him. He was walking toward me. He is Jim in this book. Jim taught me that I need to give something in return for the interview and photographs. Wanting to treat this documentary with dignity and integrity, I began to bring bags of food and blankets and to ask permission to share the stories and photos.

This was the start of a journey that I will never forget. I met people on the streets, at parks, through volunteering at New Hope Pantry and serving food at Center of Grace Outreach Center, introductions of pastors at churches. I interviewed and photographed the homeless at McDonalds, Subway, parks, Center of Grace, and on the streets.

Special thanks to my mother, Mary Brooks, and David Helton. Without them, this book would not have been possible.

Jim

"~~I'm~~ a mason by trade."

Jim

Jim proudly gave me his name. "I just lost my job. I don't know this city and don't know where to go next. I headed for the library." That is where Jim and I talked, outside the library. He had a pair of work boots around his neck, a backpack, a duffle bag, and his jacket. "This is all I own. I'm a Mason by trade."

I let Jim know he could get a hot meal at Center of Grace. He didn't know where that was. I gave him the address plus directions.

When we parted he headed into the library.

Howard

"Most people are afraid of me."

Howard

Howard just lost his job and lives mostly in his truck with his two dogs, Whitie and Alaska. "I have to sit outside for our interview. I don't like to be around a lot of people." He served in the Army from 1969 to 1971 where he recieved a Bronze Star. Since he doesn't have a permanent address he doesn't have the Bronze Star.

"He says angrily."

"Most people are afraid of me." Howard says with a tear in his eye. "I know I have PTSD"

I could not touch the dogs when we started our interview. By the end I was allowed to pet them. Howard walked me to my car and made me put on my seatbelt before he walked away.

Joe (Sarge)

"Sleeps in the wood of Olathe. He survived Desert Shield, Desert Storm, Afghanistan"

Joe (Sarge)

Sleeps in the wood of Olathe. He survived Desert Shield, Desert Storm, Afghanistan plus 6 months recovering from his wound in Walter Reed Medical center.

"I went for help at one of the local churches and was told by the receptionist that I would go to hell for killing people while in the Military." Tearfully he continued, "I was following orders."

Joe wants people to know, "Vets are returning home to no jobs!" Before Joe enlisted he was a land surveyor. "People are putting Vets — homeless Vets, down." Joe continued, "Laying outside at night, I relive some of what I went through in the Military. I have dreams of being attacked while in the Fox hole. I just want to sleep. I am so tired!"

Jeremy

"I got out of the Marines a month and a half ago. Now I am sleeping in the woods."

Jeremy

"I got out of the Marines a month and a half ago. Now I am sleeping in the woods." Jeremy explains as he holds his head in his hands. "I miss my boys. Their mother won't let me see them. I have a drinking problem. I spent 12 years protecting my men in Iraq and Afghanistan. That is why I check on Sarge and several other homeless men. I am looking for work. I had a job at a Mexican restaurant but couldn't do the work. My job before I went into the Marines was in Supply Chain Management."

Jeremy wants people to know that "A person's looks don't mean they are homeless. Homeless does not mean they are unshaven. Cleanliness is important to me. I don't ask for money, I don't ask for money."

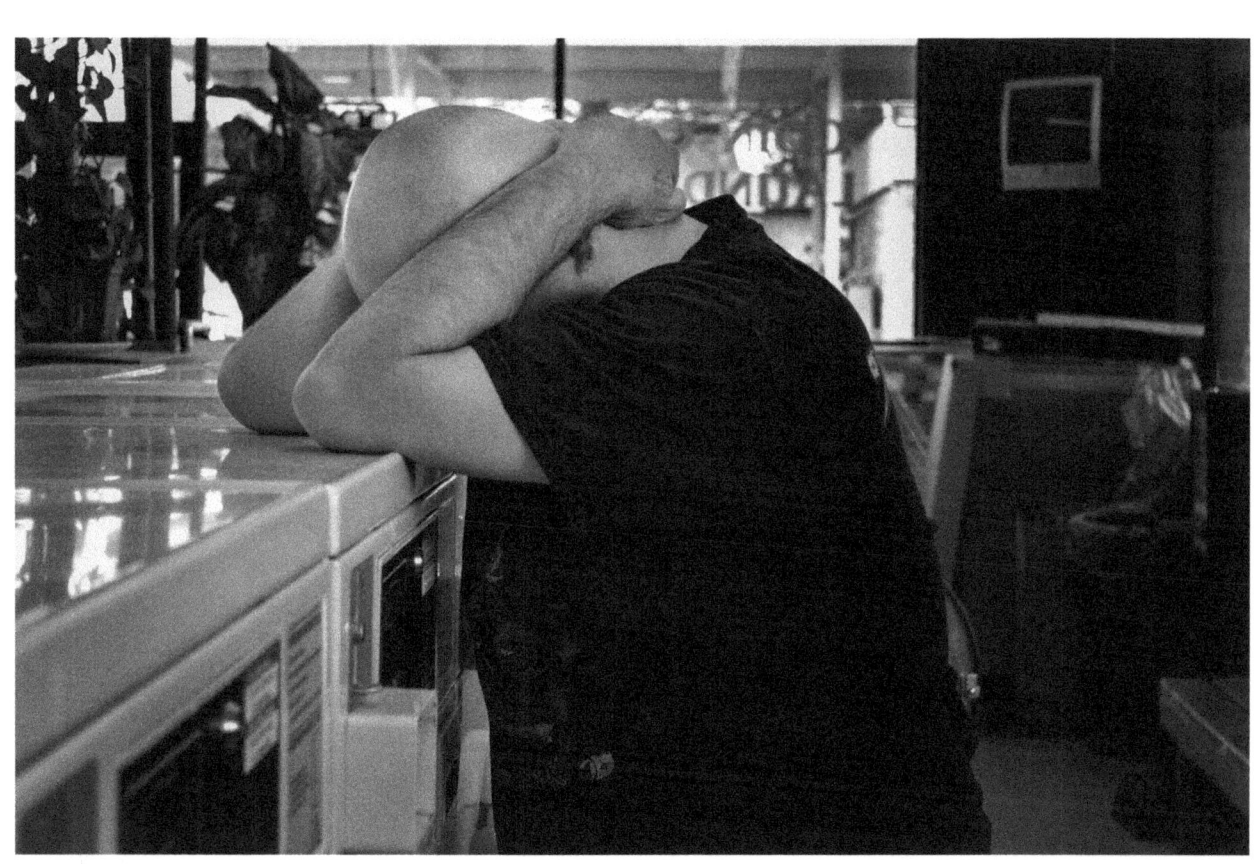

Vince

"I wish I could argue with my mom now!"

Vince

"I never thought this would happen to me." Vince says in our interview. "I took things for granted" he says as he lowers his head. At age 19 he was kicked out of his Mothers home. Then out of an Uncles home.

Vince continues, "I wish I could argue with my mom now!" It is sad to live in my Surburban. I cried the first few nights. I thought I would wake up in my house. I argued a lot with my mom."

Vince brought a couple grand with him to Kansas City. This did not last long because of the amount of money it took for gas in the Surburban.

"I sleep in parking lots of different stores. I have lost my faith but not my hope." "Now all I think about is money."

Terri and Bradley

"Smile at me."

Terri and Bradley

Terri age 24 + Bradley age 26 met at work. They fell in love. A falling out with the boss, because he wanted to date Terri, both were let go from their jobs.

They are now homeless & looking for new jobs. Terri slept on the park bench all night while Bradley stayed awake to protect her. Bradley composed a poem. A testiment of his love for Terri. Bradley says, "Terri is housewife material." Terri agrees.

Bradley continues by saying, "We don't hold a sign or beg for money."

Terri wants people to know, "Treat people the way you would want to be treated."

Bradley says, "Smile at me. I hate the way people treat the homeless — we had lives before we became homeless." Bradley continues, "I want a job so I can take care of Terri. So she can be a housewife."

Bradley's Poem to Terri

In this spot layed a woman of a young man's Dreams. He tried to think and Plot his sceams as he looks up he sees all the chared Burned Leafs. Life doesn't Really start till the verry End It seams, an he takes this time to reflect an unwind, Thinks About his Life An Relies Hes all most out of time, hes Ben Robed of Everything. An love is his Biggest Crim! So to have Loved an Lost is better than to never Loved at All!

So when that phone rings please risk it up an answer that call!!!...

IN This Spot,, LAYED A woman OF A young
man's Dreams. He Tried to Think and Put his seat as
as he Looks up he sees All the Scared Burried Leafs
as he Looked AT The woman an says
Life doesn't REALY

START Till Tho Very End iT seams,
An he TAKES This TIME To REFLECT
An unWENDs, Thinks About his FliVE
An RELISS HE's All mosT OUT OF TIME
HES BEN ROBED OF EVERYTHING
HE LOVE

IS his BIGEST CRIM! So To HAVE LOVED
An LOST is beTER Than to never LOVED
AT All! So when That Phone rings
PlEASE PICK IT up an anser

THAT CAll!!!

Herbert

"I want to share what is going on with me."

Herbert

Herbert rides his bicycle around Overland Park. There are at least 10 plastic grocery bags hanging on the bicycle. "I was living in a house in Kansas City, MO until I was kicked out. Now I am homeless." Herbert says as he moves his sunglasses down the bridge of his nose. "I am a carpenter by trade." Herbert was grateful to talk to me. When I offered him food he picked through the bag to take just what he needed. "I just went to the store." He says. "I want to share what is going on with me." Herbert says. "I don't want to keep moving." He said finally.

M. C.

"Our communication was non-verbal."

M. C.

Walking the perimeter of the tennis court in the center of downtown Olathe is a man who is dressed in the same clothes everyday. He carries two bags with his belongings. On the bags sit while he walks. Our communication was non-verbal. I dropped off a bag of food for him. A few days later I stopped at the park and saw he was carrying the bag. Then I brought my camera to the park. He let me take photos of him.

I felt that he had given me permission to take his photos when he started to carry the bag. He would not look directly at the camera but he wouldn't run from it either.

James

"It is a secret place."

James

"It is a secret place," James says when asked where he is living. He continues saying, "I'm living in a semi-truck in a court yard. The owner don't ask for anything. Because I was in so many high schools, I have a 10th grade education. I can't be bought or sold. That is why I can't find work. I fill out applications to make other people happy. People need to know my word is good. I had a much nicer computer before I went to jail. I didn't want to go to court so I went to jail. I have repaired the hard drive in one of my computers. People know my word is good. I need a stable home — somewhere I can create, a place of respect, and comfort. There are no homeless shelters in the area. Somehow I know it will all work out."

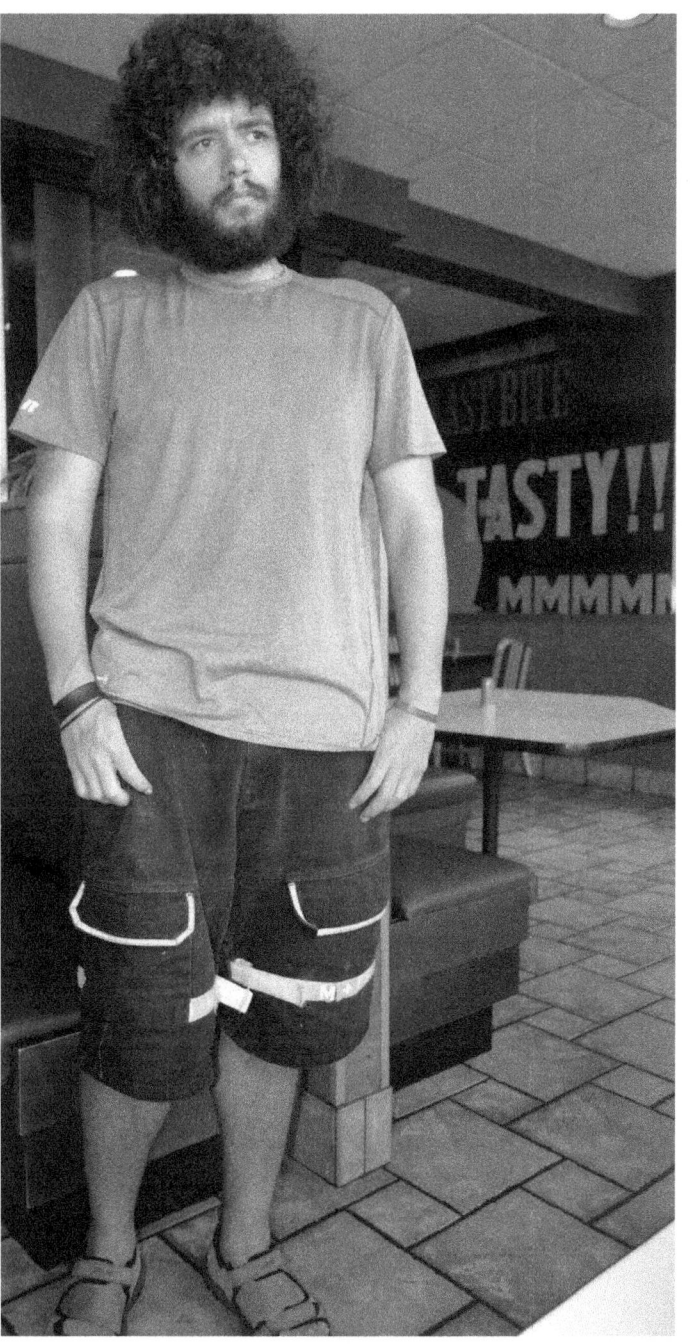

Randi & Lester

"We are not here because we want to be."

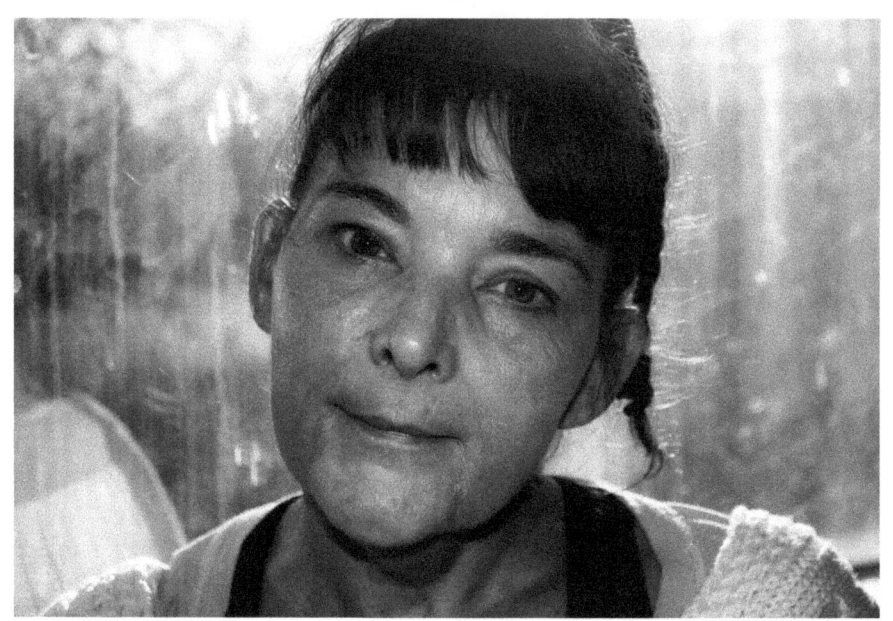

Randi & Lester

"We have been married for 23 years. We are not here because we want to be. It is more expensive to be homeless" Randi says. They now live in their car after accumulating an overwhelming amount of medical bills. Lester is 52 yrs old, Randi is 50 yrs old. "Lester had a heart attack when we lived in a motel. We had medical bills from my surgeries before that. Lester walked our daughter to sleep when she was a baby. I volunteered at our childrens schools. I was even my sons soccer coach. Now we need a place to live so we can take care of our children. Our daughter is a sophmore in college. Our son is in foster care. Homeless is the worse thing I been through. Don't turn away from the homeless."

Youlanda

"I am a survivor"

Youlanda

"There is always a way out by finding a Higher Power. I tried to stop doing drugs & prostitution on my own. I couldn't do it. That life didn't work for me. I was riding buses to stay warm. I was staying all night in casino's to be safe. Now I have my own apartment. I was in a safe home in Missouri when I was connected to Johnson County Mental Health. My husband got me on drugs. Then I started prostitution. My mental problems started with the beatings while I was a prostitue. Now I am 7 months clean & sober. I go to programs & meetings to help me. I want to do volunteer work to give back. When I am clean & sober I can meet my responsibilities. I am a survivor!"

Shawn

"There are hateful people out there. Boo Boo is my protector."

Shawn

"I have been homeless for 2 years. I'm in my 40's. Before I became homeless I was a handyman. I'm carrying Boo Boo's food in my backpack."

Shawn was walking with Boo Boo in 30 degree weather.

"I want people to come together to help us homeless out. I don't need anything. I sleep in a secret place. There are hateful people out there. Boo Boo is my protector."

I could not pet Boo Boo because I could not get close to him & Shawn. When we finished Shawn continued proudly walking down the street!

Bike Rider

"He knew
I was following him
and he lost me."

Bike Rider

Riding a bike though the streets of Olathe is a man wearing a chiefs jacket that is tattered and torn. It can be 20° or 90° he is still in that coat. I first saw him in the parking lot of Little Ceasars. He had bags with his belonging on the handle bars of the bike.

The rider is often seen getting food from people at McDonalds next to Little Ceasars. I followed him in hopes of talking to him.

He led me though the back streets of Olathe. He knew I was following him and he lost me.

Notes from the Community ...

"Homelessness is not part of the 'chosen' identity of Johnson County, Kansas. Poverty does not 'jibe' with the Money magazine image of one of the best places to live, retire or raise your children. A problem denied is a problem unsolved. The antidote to denial is acknowledgement. One way to move the dialogue forward is to witness the truth. One way to acknowledge and understand is to see the faces of the individuals whose lives are lived without resources and a safe place to sleep. What Sharon has done is to respectfully visit, give her time, make friends and document the voices and visage of people in our county who live homeless. These people are not invisible, they are not silent, they are ignored and denied."

--Nicole Emanuel
founder InterUrban ArtHouse, KS

"Sharon cares about people, and it shows in these images. But documentary photography is not just about a camera. You don't make pictures like this without trust. And when people live a precarious life, trust can be illusive. Sharon stepped off the beaten path - literally - to engage understandably cautious, even fearful, strangers in an unknown environment - in a sense walking right into their homes. If you don't exude respect, sincerity and caring in an instant this can have undesirable consequences. But Sharon does. Her heart and deference invite conversation, and from there a bond is made. I am engaged by each face. I see their life in their eyes and the place they call home."

--Mark Berndt
photographer, NM

WHAT YOU CAN DO

1.   Homelessness is an unpleasant subject. It is scary to know what to do. Talk about it with family friends and co-workers to build awareness. You can't know what to do if you ignore the issues. When I told people about this project, the common response was, "I didn't know we had homeless in Johnson County."

2.   Find reputable agencies that help the homeless. In Johnson County that is Salvation Army; Catholic Charities, Center of Grace outreach, Southside Mission, Redeemer Church, New Hope Food Pantry to name a few. These are some of the ones I worked with during this project.

3.   Carry food or clothing. When you meet a homeless person make eye contact and smile. Don't look away. They are people, too. I personally will give food or clothing to them.

4.   Know the agencies in your area and what they do so that when you do meet a homeless person you can give them references. I found out that Salvation Army in Olathe has a shower facility open in the afternoon to the homeless. Sometimes a shower is all they want. Or clean socks.

Sharon Rodriguez

-photo by Bill Mitchell

"Each photograph has a story to tell. I tell what I see and invite the viewer to look at the work and tell the story they see."

Sharon Rodriguez is a photographer living and working in Olathe, Kansas. Her photographic documentary work focuses on the exploration of marginalized communities. This book is the culmination of the previous two years work with homeless individuals in the affluent suburb of Olathe. The photos have been featured at the Lackman Branch of the Johnson County Library in an exhibit entitled "Shining the Light on the Homeless of Johnson County," part of the "Bear Witness" exhibition sequence which explores art as activism. Rodriguez is a mother and grandmother and can be reached at srodriguez22@att.net.

www.ingramcontent.com/pod-product-compliance
Lightning Source LLC
Chambersburg PA
CBHW061930290426
44113CB00024B/2868